Everything
I Need to Know
I Learned in
Sunday School

Everything I Need to Know I Learned in Sunday School

• Keeping Focused on the Basics •

David Shibley

New Leaf Press

Table of Contents

Assuredly, I say to you,
whoever does not receive
the kingdom of God
as a little child
will by no means enter it

(Luke 18:17).

Creation in Flannelgraph

The light blue flannelboard was bare. Being a boy, I wasn't too interested in the fabric that covered the board. I just remembered that it looked a lot like the same stuff they wrapped the baby Jesus doll in for the Christmas play.

But in my mind's eye that morning, the board turned pitch black as Mrs. King whispered the passage out of Genesis, "And *darkness* covered the face of the deep."

Suddenly, seemingly out of nowhere (just like creation), a flannelgraph sun burst rays of brilliant light all over the board. "And God said, 'Let there be *light!*' " Mrs. King had a way of making the creation story really come alive.

Suddenly, pastel colored flowers sprang up in dramatic relief against the backdrop. Majestic mountains and flowing streams appeared. Then beautiful animals.

And, then, there they were — the crowning glory of God's creation, Adam and Eve (tastefully sheltered behind a bush, of course). As I stared at my great, great, etc. grandparents, Mrs. King was saying something about how very special each of us children were because we were made in the image of God. She said that people were more beautiful to God than the prettiest flower, more precious than anything else He had made. Then Mrs. King reminded us that the Bible says we are "fearfully and wonderfully made."

Because God had made the earth and everything in it, we were to take good care of all He had made. Because God had made all people in His very image, we were valuable. We should value ourselves and we should value and respect all other people, too.

This cardinal truth was reinforced by my teacher (yes, in *public* school) when she taught us to recite:

> *All things bright and beautiful,*
> *All creatures great and small,*
> *All things wise and wonderful,*
> *The Lord God made them all.*
> —Cecil Frances Alexander

All I need to know I learned in Sunday school. It was there I learned to respect and revere all that God created. Based on what I learned there I understood that God values *all* people; all races, all classes, the weak, and those who are so powerless they cannot defend themselves. In Sunday school I learned that *people matter, because they are made in the image of God.*

Sadly, Lord,
times have changed.
Intrinsic human dignity is no
longer affirmed in many public schools.
Evolution has eroded that. But Your
Word hasn't changed. People still matter to
You. Help me always to remember that. Put
Your heart in me so that people always
matter to me, too. In the name of
Jesus, who died because people
matter. Amen.

Wide, Wide as the Ocean

Today they might call it aerobics. At least it was good stretching exercises. Happy little girls in dresses with can-cans. Little boys with bow ties and suspenders. Stretching as wide as we could span our little pipe arms. Reaching up as high as possible. Bending down to touch the floor. And all to illustrate with elegant simplicity as we sang:

> *Wide, wide as the ocean,*
> *High as the heavens above,*
> *Deep, deep as the deepest sea*
> *Is my Saviour's love.*
>
> *Though I'm so unworthy,*
> *Still I'm a child of His care.*
> *For His Word teaches me*
> *That His love reaches me*
> *Everywhere.*

When I rehearse that chorus, even today, a deep warmth goes through me. As we sang it in Sunday school years ago, we surely experienced the same sensation as Robert Browning when he penned, "God's in His heaven

And Jesus said, "Let the little children come to Me, and do not forbig them; for of such is the kingdom of heaven

(Matt. 19:14).

— all's right with the world."

Just imagine! God's love for me was as wide and deep as the Gulf of Mexico I'd seen last summer on our family vacation. Even though I didn't deserve it, Jesus *cared* about *me*. What a deep sense of security and worth was being woven into me as I sang. And then to recite our memory verse: "For He himself has said, 'I will *never* leave you nor forsake you' " (Heb. 13:5). As our teacher said, "Never, never, *never!*"

God's love for me was (in a word I would learn later) *unconditional*. The dimensions of His love were immeasurable. The consequences of His love brought joy unspeakable.

A simple song and an accompanying verse. But, you tell me — what could possibly be a richer heritage than the truth I tucked away in my heart that day?

▲▲▲▲▲▲

In later years, life's blows would challenge that little song. Disappointments would assault His promise. Yet, tougher than life's most brutal blows, deeper than the disappointments — there His love is still. It was in Sunday school that day that I caught hold of one of life's most important truths: No matter how far you run, no matter how rough your circumstances, *you can never run away from God's love.*

*Your Word
declares it, and my heart
knows it: God is love. Thank You
for loving me, through my rebellion, past
my heartaches, loving me up-close and
silent when my dull logic thought You were a
million miles away. Almost 50 years now, Lord,
and Your love still stretches wider, deeper,
higher than I can ever explore. But thank You
for the joy of trying to find its limits. Thank
You for the deep peace that was bred into
me because my parents and my teachers
taught me (and showed me) that
Your love knows no
bounds. Amen.*

A Friend of Sinners

Nobody had to convince me I was a sinner. And no "enlightened" liberal theologian could have talked me out of my guilt. Even as a child, I had an enormous propensity for doing the wrong thing!

My dad was a conscientious, conservative pastor. He was assiduous not to cause offense or harm the gospel in any way. Smoking and drinking, even when he was a sailor, were completely foreign to him. So you can imagine his response when he discovered I was standing at the door of our church one Sunday morning, greeting each person with this pronouncement: "My daddy smokes big, black cigars!"

That afternoon I learned a very pointed, painful lesson about the wages of sin. I was reminded in no uncertain terms that one of God's "big ten" is, "Thou shalt not bear false witness."

And then there's another incident from "church history" that comes to mind. My dad would sometimes transmit live radio broadcasts from the church, complete with the choir singing in the background. But while Dad was "reaching the masses through the miracle of radio," my buddies and I were playing tag all around the church property. In the thrill of the

chase I forgot two incontestable rules: Never run in church and always maintain absolute silence during the broadcast. In the middle of the choir's anthem, I burst through the side door, yelling to my friends outside, "I bet you'll never catch me now!"

They didn't . . . but my father did. The next thing I recall was icy fear. Dad and I were walking to a secluded spot behind the church. Off came his belt. Down came my pants. Verily, I was a sinner. A sinner under judgment.

But then something incredible happened. The sting in my posterior and the embarrassment in my heart was being drowned by big arms that were embracing me. And a strong, comforting voice that said he forgave me. And then, in the backseat with my giggling sisters, we were driving home. But Dad wanted to make one stop first.

"Son, how about an ice cream cone?"

Excuse me, Dad? Are you talking to me — the reprobate who just made his unrehearsed radio debut? But he was addressing me — not my well-behaved sisters, but the old sinner-boy. (Much the same as when Jesus came first looking for the turncoat, Peter, after His resurrection.)

His voice again broke through my thoughts. "Son, would you like some ice cream?" I couldn't believe it — he was acting *like my episode never happened!*

Come to think of it, that's what my Sunday school teacher said it meant to be *justified* — "just as if I'd never sinned."

The Church today is peppered with self-righteous people who have little time for sinners. It seems that the American church has adopted a perennially adversarial posture. People seeking answers are often met with about as much warmth and welcome as I was when I made my unexpected entrance. (Folks who come into church unexpectedly are often not well received.) How antithetical to the reception from Jesus: Jesus is for people, *Jesus is a friend of sinners*. Yes, Jesus loves me. The Bible tells me so. I learned that in Sunday school.

I still marvel,
Lord, (as well I should) at
how Your love embraces us
sinners. That kind of forgiving,
healing love is so out of character for us
and so completely in character for You. But
when we get to know You, that kind of love
is shed abroad in our hearts, too, by Your
Spirit. I know You are a friend of sinners
because You are a friend of mine.
Make me a friend of sinners, too.
In Your name. Amen.

The Wordless Book

It was my turn to flip the pages in the big book with the green cover. I turned the four pages of the book while the rest of the kids sang out heartily.

The book in my hand was the big version of an interesting, miniature book. This was a book without words; in fact, we called it the *Wordless Book*. The first page was black as night. The second page, crimson red. The third page was pure white and the fourth page was gold. I've since learned that the gold page was a pretty sophisticated printing accomplishment for the 1950s.

And so we sang,

> *My heart was dark with sin,*
> *Until the Saviour came in.*
> *His precious blood, I know,*
> *Has washed me white as snow.*
> *And in His Word I'm told*
> *I'll walk the streets of gold.*
> *Oh, wonderful, wonderful day!*
> *He washed my sins away.*

Then I closed the book, exposing the green cover. Again we sang,

> *To grow in Christ each day,*
> *I read my Bible and pray.*

Gospel basics. Treasured, timeless, gospel basics. Later I would learn more "adult" presentations of the gospel: *The Four Spiritual Laws,* the "Roman Road" and Evangelism Explosion. Although they are fuller explanations, they all are essentially commentaries on the four-line *Wordless Book* rhyme.

Later, in high school, I'd make contact with Youth for Christ and the Navigators. I got familiar with Dawson Trotman's "wheel": Christ is the hub; obedience the rim; and the Word, prayer, witness, and fellowship were the spokes. Again, it was just a little fuller explanation of the green cover.

Don't tell me you can't make profound theology simple. The great old Baptist preacher Vance Havner was right when he observed, "It's about time we gave up all this theological grand opera and went back to practicing the scales."

Perhaps that's why Sunday school has so impacted my life. Over and over, we practiced those beautiful, precision scales on which the rest of the music of life is built. Winston Churchill said, "All great things are simple, and many can be expressed in a single word: freedom; justice; honor; duty; mercy; hope." May I add to Mr. Churchill's impressive list another great word: *salvation.*

And that makes me want to tell you about my most wonderful, wonderful day.

▲▲▲▲▲▲

As I write this book, *God's Little Book* on this and that subject are enormously popular. In fact, I've written one myself.* But perhaps God's "little book" we need most is a massive redistribution of the *Wordless Book.* The nectar of the gospel in four pages: man's sin, Christ's sacrifice, the believer's cleansing, and eternity with God.

Challenging Quotes for World Changers, (Green Forest, AR: New Leaf Press, 1995).

I'm so
grateful, Lord, that the
most profound truths can be
embraced even by children. I grow in
the implications of these truths daily. But
I'm thankful that faith makes them em-
braceable and makes their benefits personal.
I know that all truth is Your truth. And
I'm forever grateful that early on my
parents and teachers put Your
truth in my heart.
Amen

June 12, 1953

I still have "snapshot" recollections of that pivotal day. The warm Oklahoma sun was shining as my pre-school legs scaled the steps up to the front door of Beams of Light Church in Tulsa. This was church just for us kids — Vacation Bible School!

I remember what appeared to be hundreds of kids, singing songs to Jesus, including this one:

> *Into my heart, Into my heart,*
> *Come into my heart, Lord Jesus.*
> *Come in today. Come in to stay.*
> *Come into my heart, Lord Jesus.*

The next "snapshot" I recall is Mrs. Gertrude Nathan, looking like the quintessential VBS teacher in her wire rim glasses, telling the old, old story. In the next frame, somehow I had left my seat. I'm kneeling at an old-time altar at the front, and Mrs. Nathan is leading us in that eternity-altering prayer:

> *Lord Jesus, thank You for dying on the cross*
> *for me. Right now, I turn away from all my sins.*
> *Come into my heart, Lord Jesus. Take my sins away.*

I want to be Your child from now on. Help me to live for You all the days of my life. Amen.

Twenty-five years later, in seminary, a professor grilled me on the legitimacy of that conversion. He was convinced that children have, as he called it, a "volitional impediment" that prevents them from making such monumental decisions.

"Tell me," my professor said, "that day when you say you were saved, did you understand the implications of the atonement?"

"No," I replied. "Do you?" What adult can fully comprehend the rationale or the magnitude of redemption? We need only believe and receive the gospel.

It's quite clear that Madison Avenue knows of no such "volitional impediment" in the very young. Christians seem to be the only ones who believe they should wait to influence children's minds. Advertisers don't wait. Child abusers don't wait. Occult-riddled cartoons that drench Saturday morning TV don't wait. The devil himself doesn't wait. America's children today do not suffer from overexposure to Jesus but from underexposure to Him.

Fortunately for most of us, the Bible does not say, "Exegete the gospel and you will be saved." It doesn't even

24

say, "Comprehend the implications of the gospel and you will be saved." The Bible simply says, "Believe on the Lord Jesus Christ and you will be saved."

And even a child can do that, *especially* a child can do that. Jesus explicitly said, "Allow the *little* children to come to Me. Do not forbid them, for of such is the kingdom of heaven."

That glorious day, I believed.

In this case, it was in Vacation Bible School, a first cousin to Sunday school, where I took to heart life's greatest advice: *Open your heart to Jesus.*

A few years ago, I was back at that very church where 40 years earlier I first had opened my heart to Christ. I walked into the auditorium in the afternoon, when no one was there. It looks much the same as in 1953. I walked to the front and knelt at the altar, at the very place where my life had been so wonderfully changed. I just knelt in worship, thanking God again for so great salvation. And then I made a fresh commitment that I would spend the rest of my life getting what happened to me there . . . to others. And that brings me to our next story.

I'm forever

grateful, Lord Jesus, that the

gospel reached me early in life. Thank

You for the work of Your Spirit in me that

prompted me to open my young heart wide

to You. Thank You for Gertrude Nathan

and thousands like her who faithfully

point the little children to

You. Amen.

A Wonderful Way to Spell "Joy"

A few years ago, some folks caused quite a stir by urging people to "commit random acts of kindness." I recall that this injunction was labeled as "fresh and new."

The concept might have been novel to some, but it's nothing new to those privileged to have sat through Sunday school. Some of my earliest recollections are of the Golden Rule, Jesus' simple, earthshaking teaching that we are to "do unto others as you would have them do unto you."

Then, there's much talk today about priorities. No time management seminar is complete without the preachment, "Get your priorities in order!" Again, for us Sunday schoolers, we learned the proper sequence of priorities years ago:

> *Jesus, others, and you:*
> *What a wonderful way to spell joy!*

Jesus first. Later that concept would be expanded for me in the beautiful didactic of the Westminster Shorter Catechism: "What is the sole purpose of man? The sole purpose of man is to glorify God and enjoy Him forever."

Life's focus was first to be vertical. We exist for *His* pleasure, not ours. Or, as one of my early memory verses says, "And whatever you do in word or deed, do all in the name of the Lord Jesus, giving thanks to God the Father through Him" (Col. 3:17).

People second. A close second. For we bring glory to God by honoring and lifting those creatures uniquely made in His image — men and women.

A wealthy philanthropist once offered to telegraph a sermon of William Booth, the founder of the Salvation Army, around the world. "But there's one stipulation, Mr. Booth," he cautioned. "Your sermon can be only one word long."

Booth immediately accepted the offer. William Booth's one-word, worldwide-telegraphed sermon was a masterpiece. Here it is: *"Others."*

General Booth embraced the Lord's philosophy of ministry: "For even the Son of Man did not come to be served, but to serve, and to give His life a ransom for many" (Mark 10:45).

Yourself third. A distant third. When we dive into the deep end of the pool of people's needs, and when we live for God's glory alone, it's amazing how our own struggles fade and sometimes even disappear.

"Joy" is spelled, "Jesus, others, and you." What a bright, innovative idea. Except for us "privileged kids" who went to Sunday school.

▲▲▲▲▲▲

Today we talk in terms of "self-fulfillment" and "self-actualization." Not that long ago, Christians spoke about "self-sacrifice." Isn't it interesting that those who learn self-sacrifice end up being far more fulfilled and actualized than those who try to spell "joy" some other way?

Years ago, C.S. Lewis described it as being "surprised by joy." Yet, as profound as this joy spawned by servanthood seems to us, Lord, it's no surprise to You. You taught us so plainly, "For whoever desires to save his life will lose it, but whoever loses his life for My sake and the gospel's will save it." I buy that in principle. Help me to live it out today in "random acts of kindness" that are prompted by Your life in me. In Jesus' name, for Your sake and the gospel's. Amen.

Barrel Barney

The south side of Tulsa in the 1950s was a pretty sheltered place. My first encounter with kids in need wasn't face to face. It was in a story from Sunday school.

Mrs. King was putting the figure of an old barrel on the flannelgraph. Then she told us the story of a boy just about my age named Barney. Barney didn't know where or who his parents were. (That was shock treatment; I thought *every* kid lived with his parents.)

As if that weren't enough, Barney didn't have a home to live in. No home? I thought *every* kid went to a place each night where he was sheltered, fed, and loved.

But not Barney. For shelter, Mrs. King explained as she slid the figure of a little boy inside the barrel, Barney went home at night to his barrel.

Could there really be kids like that? Lovingly, Mrs. King assured us there were. Well, then, something had to be done about this! Mrs. King told us we could make a difference, one child at a time.

I no longer remember all the particulars of Barrel Barney's story. I remember he became ill because he lived outside in the

*From childhood you have known
the Holy Scriptures, which are
able to make you wise for salvation through faith which is in
Christ Jesus*
(2 Tim. 3:15).

cold. I remember loving Christians took him in, gave him his first warm bed, and told him about Jesus.

I also remember that Barney died. But before he died, he invited Jesus into his heart. The last mental image I remember was of Barrel Barney in heaven. He had left the "wrong side of the tracks" for a city of unspeakable splendor. No longer friendless, he was meeting throngs of new brothers and sisters. And now, because of Jesus, the little boy who had lived in a barrel lived in a mansion.

Years have passed. God has allowed me the privilege of ministering in over 40 nations. I've met many of the world's "Barrel Barney's." I've talked with street kids in Sao Paulo, as they tried to stay warm under pieces of cardboard. I've held malnourished orphans in India. My eyes have met with the empty stares of refugee children in Lebanon. For children, the world is an increasingly savage place.

What Barney finally received is what each child deserves. Children need the compassionate touch of those who care. They need the gospel and its liberating effects. They need hope. Government aid may provide necessities that will prolong existence; only people can bring love and hope.

I learned that in Sunday school.

AAAAAA

    When a wealthy Christian businessman named Robert Raikes founded Sunday schools in 1780, it was because he wanted to help kids like Barrel Barney. Raikes went into the slums of the cities, gathering the poorest kids in town in order to get them under the sound of the gospel. Today, people like Bill Wilson in New York follow in Raikes' footsteps. Sunday school still works. Because the gospel still works.

Father in heaven,
I lift my voice today in behalf of
the Barrel Barneys of our sin-drenched
world. These precious children stare at
poverty and lack everyday. It's our fault, Lord.
Forgive us, Lord, for the greed that helped
produce these conditions and the indifference
that allows them to continue to exist. As my
arteries tend to harden, dear Jesus, make
my heart softer and more like Yours.
There are plenty of activists
with lesser

All the Children of the World

"Eenie, meenie, miney, moe. Catch a _____ by his toe!"

We'd been having a great time playing in our neighborhood. All of a sudden, though, I felt sick. "What did they just say?"

"NO!," I shouted back, my face turning red. "It's catch a *tiger* by his toe." The other kids laughed and one of them yelled back, "No, it's not. It's catch a _____!"

I probably had never heard the word *prejudice*. I couldn't have spelled it. But I experienced it vicariously that day in my insular, all-white world.

My heart was still pounding. My face was flushed. "How could they *say* that? Don't they know how it hurts people?" They knew, all right.

Those kids probably meant nothing sinister. It was just the same old game, with the same demeaning words their parents had played years before. But what caused me to make such a big deal of their stupid little rhyme?

Maybe it had something to do with how deeply I believed that song we sang so often in Sunday school:

Jesus loves the little children,
All the children of the world.
Red, brown, yellow, black, and white,
All are precious in His sight.
Jesus loves the little children
Of the world.

How much better would our world be if everyone (including adults, *especially* adults) sang and believed that song? What if the black kids in the city, the white kids in the suburbs, the Hispanic kids, the Chinese kids, the Indian kids sang that song, not only *about* each other but *with* each other?

The purpose-driven missionary who came to our church underscored the truth of that song when he cried, "Why should anyone hear the gospel twice until everyone has heard it once?"

My parents and Sunday school teachers reinforced it when they taught us the Bible, compressed in one majestic verse: "For God so loved the world that He gave His only begotten Son, that whoever believes in Him should not perish but have everlasting life" (John 3:16).

Fidelity to that truth has been a driving force to my commitment to missions work. Very early my family and church impressed on me that *God doesn't play favorites.* "Liberty and justice for all." Before I heard that in public school, I had already embraced it in Sunday school.

▲▲▲▲▲▲

Several years later in college, I watched a soft drink ad on TV. A vast, multi-ethnic choir caroling something about teaching the world to sing in perfect harmony. And the inference that it all began with a shared trans-cultural bottle of that beverage. Now, I like that particular soft drink as much as the next guy. But I'm convinced that the only hope for global harmony is not in a bottle but in the Bible. And our product is every bit as cross-cultural and far more beneficial. "Oh, taste and see that the Lord is good" (Ps. 34:8).

A few years ago,
Lord, I thought we were
making progress against racism. But
now it seems our nation is racked with
more ethnic strife than at any time since the
Civil War. Raise up a new generation who
will live out the truth that Your love knows
no boundaries — social, racial, national,
or economic. Heal us. Mend us.
Spread Your love through us,
Lord Jesus. Amen.

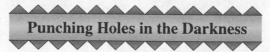

Punching Holes in the Darkness

There are perhaps few more serene scenes of tranquillity than a bright Sunday morning with the sweet voices of children singing in the background:

> *Jesus wants me for a sunbeam,*
> *To shine for Him each day.*
> *In everything try to please Him,*
> *At home, at school, at play.*
>
> *A sunbeam, a sunbeam,*
> *Jesus wants me for a sunbeam.*
> *A sunbeam, a sunbeam;*
> *I'll be a sunbeam for Him.*

That song was a standard in the repertoire of the Canary Choir, as our kids' chorus was affectionately dubbed.

Later I'd learn that it is better to light a candle than merely to curse the darkness. But I wasn't more than three years old when I found out that even a little light that is lifted high enough can illumine the darkness. We promised as we sang that we wouldn't hide our light under a bushel, but that we'd shine it 'round the neighborhood, even shine it 'round the whole wide world. And we'd "let it shine till Jesus comes."

We could be sunbeams for Him, even when things looked pretty gloomy. When I was a teenager I saw that lived out in the life of my dad. Fatigue and disease had vastly limited this once physically powerful man. For a time during his illness, he would sit on the front porch of our home for hours, endeavoring to recover his strength.

It wasn't a happy time. Our family wondered about our future. Dad was literally fighting for his life (a fight he eventually lost). Although I was still in Sunday school, I wasn't a little kid anymore. But I watched the little kids in our neighborhood, remembering how I, too, used to be carefree just a few years earlier.

The little kids on our block began to look for my dad, as he would watch them play from our porch. Dad never got to go to Bible college; World War II interrupted those plans. He was a pastor without a degree, but, in my book, a pastor without peer. My father did, however, receive one coveted title. The theological community would never call him a "doctor of divinity." But the kids in our neighborhood dubbed him "the sunshine man." Even in his pain, Jesus shone through.

I can see it in my mind even now, typed on bold letters on strips of paper, with felt backs to stick to the flannelgraph. We learned it one phrase at a time:

> **Let your light so shine before men,**
> **that they may see your good works**
> **and glorify your Father in heaven**
> **(Matt. 5:16).**

▲▲▲▲▲▲

A little boy in Victorian England was walking down the sidewalk with his father at dusk. The lamplighter was patiently lighting each lamppost, one wick at a time. "Look, Father," the little boy exuded, "that man's punching holes in the darkness!"

In the same way, no matter how somber the circumstances, you can be used by Jesus as a shaft of light, piercing the darkness. Today, in the normal traffic patterns of your life, *you can spread the sunshine of God's love*. It's an insight I picked up in Sunday school.

I have no trouble,
Lord, believing that You are the
Light of the world. What I find
troubling is Your statement to me: "You
are the light of the world." There's only one
way that can be true — by reflection. So,
shine, Jesus, shine! Shine Your light to me, in
every dark corner of my life. Then shine Your
light through me, to every dark corner of
my world. For Your name's sake,
make me Your namesake —
"Christian" — like Christ.
Amen.

Have you heard the one about when little Johnny was quizzed by his Sunday school teacher?

"Johnny," the teacher inquired, "what is false doctrine?"

Misunderstanding the question, Johnny replied, "Well, I guess false doctorin' is when you give the wrong medicine to sick people."

Johnny was right, in more ways than one. Unfortunately, there's a lot of false doctorin' out there these days. Faulty diagnoses. Bad prescriptions. Quack cures. And all because of false doctorin'! When I was growing up, "the Bible says" meant "end of argument." There was never any doubt when we sang: "The B-I-B-L-E. Yes, that's the book for me!" After all, how could one ever doubt *God's Word*?

I'm familiar with all the caricatures of Bible-thumping fundamentalists. My Sunday school teachers weren't Bible thumpers, they were Bible believers. And they weren't ethereal dreamers, they were clear-eyed realists, committed to the deadly serious business of building the next generation.

Not once do I recall a Sunday school teacher promising me an automatically well-lit path through life. I do recall that they told me where to go for illumination when the road was

Let the little children come to Me,
and do not forbid them; for of
such is the kingdom of God
(Mark 10:14).

hazy. "Your word is a lamp to my feet and a light to my path" (Ps. 119:105). Nor did any Sunday school teacher promise me exemption from temptation. They did counsel me, "How can a young man cleanse his way? But taking heed according to Your word. . . . Your word I have hidden in my heart, that I might not sin against You" (Ps. 119:9,11).

By the time I was in seminary, even in that school's conservative denomination, some folks seemed to choke at calling the Bible *inerrant* or *infallible*. But their false doctorin' came too late for me. You see, before some of my seminary teachers ever insinuated otherwise, my Sunday school teachers had assured me, "Forever, O Lord, Your word is settled in heaven" (Ps. 119:89). If it's settled in heaven, it's settled for me.

I'm glad I didn't have to struggle to find the basis of authority and truth when I went to college. Years earlier, in child-like faith, I had accepted the Bible as the Word of God. At the end of seminary, I realized that is still the way the Bible must be embraced, in simple faith. An anchor that never loses its moorings, even after my half-century of interacting with it, I keep learning every day that *the Bible is God's book and our faithful guide*. But I learned that first in Sunday school.

Lord Jesus, You are
the living Word. Thank You for
extending Your very essence to us
through Your infallible book. In a world
that is itself winding down, I rest in Your
promise: Heaven and earth will pass away,
but the words that You speak will never
pass away. And for this, Lord, my
heart is glad.
Amen.

One hundred sixth graders sang out in sacred harmony. Some 200 parents sat smiling and nodding their approval. Beautifully the young choir sang,

> *Fair is the sunshine,*
> *Fairer still the moonlight*
> *And all the twinkling, starry host;*
> *Jesus shines brighter,*
> *Jesus shines purer*
> *Than all the angels heaven can boast.*

The scene? No, it wasn't church. It was the monthly meeting of the John Marshall Elementary School PTA, 1960.

I take offense at hearing repeatedly how evangelical Christians have drifted away from mainstream America. I haven't "drifted" anywhere. In 1960 nobody saw a conflict of interests in what happened that night at the PTA meeting. No parent ranted about some convoluted separation of church and state. To suggest that spring night that anyone's rights had been violated would have been ridiculed as preposterous. If someone has "drifted" away from center in the last 40 years, it hasn't been us.

Back then there was no clashing of principles. The PTA supported Sunday schools. The Boy Scouts weren't much different from church camp. And in Vacation Bible School, you could count on pledging allegiance to one beloved country, one eternal kingdom, and one infallible Book.

It went without saying that a dominant Christian ethic was the very best safeguard of liberties, not only for Christians, but for Muslims, Jews, and the completely irreligious. After all, what commonly-held moral base would atheists fall back on to ensure the protection of Christians? But Christians were biblically enjoined to love and protect even those hostile to them. Remember, it was Jesus who said, "Love your enemies."

To love God meant that I loved my neighbor, and that I loved my extended neighbors as together we shared the dream that was America. And to love America properly, I should love God. For without question, God had shed His grace on this land. It was now up to conscientious citizens to "crown its good with brotherhood."

▲▲▲▲▲▲

My father was no fan of the politics of John Kennedy. But the Sunday after President Kennedy was assassinated, I caught a glimpse of what made America great. Dad was leading our congregation in a heart-wrenching prayer, asking God that "this despicable act," as he termed it, would somehow point the nation to Him. Some would imply today that conservative churches are a kind of breeding ground for subversives. But the whole Bible-believing Christian scene underscored for me that you should *serve your country by being a good citizen.* I remember that from Sunday school.

God,

have mercy on America.

Grant us the gift of repentance and

the joy of sins forgiven. In our hate-

filled nation, make us Your ministers of

reconciliation. Turn us, and we will be

turned. Heal us, and we will be healed.

Dear God, please, revive us again. For

Jesus' sake. Amen.

Loyalty to His Kingdom

Throughout history, whenever God has a big job to get done, He has often called on a young person. When it was time for national cleansing and a new sense of divine destiny, He commissioned a brash, young zealot named Gideon. When it was time to silence a blaspheming giant, He called on a shepherd boy named David. When it was time to clothe himself in humanity, He turned to a young virgin named Mary.

The pattern continues throughout Church history. William Carey launches the modern missionary movement by sailing from England to India. He would never return home. Mary Slessor single-handedly takes on the brutalities of pagan West Africa and imposes a new system of justice, based on Scripture. Jim Elliot dies, face down on a beach in Ecuador's jungle with a poison-tipped spear in his back, attempting to get the gospel to the Aucas. None of these pioneers were yet 30 years old.

Throughout my formative years, a steady stream of God's unsung heroes made their way through my Sunday school classes: a spinster-missionary who loved orphaned kids in Tunisia, a missionary pilot who landed on beaches in jungles, and a missionary to Africa who passed around native spears and shields to us wide-eyed boys.

I began to see that allegiance to that second flag, that other "country," was just as compelling as loyalty to my native land. Jesus spoke often of an eternal kingdom that was not of this world. Slowly through the years of Sunday school, I began to see that there was a cause that all this represented. I was being offered the high dignity of being an ambassador for Christ. God had a worldwide plan and I could participate in it.

Count Nikolas von Zinzendorf said, "That nation is henceforth my country which most needs the gospel." Somewhere along the way, that missions spirit caught hold of me. I was a citizen of two kingdoms. I loved America, but I came to understand I had a global responsibility. I can thank my missions-hearted parents for that. And Sunday school.

Many in Generation X lack a galvanizing purpose for their lives. It's not their fault. Their parents have almost prided themselves in espousing a painless Christianity.

We owe our kids a cause big enough and noble enough to live for and, if need be, to die for. Francis Xavier challenged the youth of his day to "give up their small ambitions and come eastward and preach the gospel of Christ." Too many Christians today have no ambitions at all. And if they have some, they're usually too small. Embrace the *Great Commission*. What a glorious way to live — free from small ambitions! In Sunday school I learned to *live for what matters, and what matters is the exaltation of the Son of God to the ends of the earth.*

Dear Father, give us more
Sunday school teachers who will dare
their students, as William Carey said, to
attempt great things for You and expect
great things from You. You deserve no less.
In the name of Jesus, Lord of all nations.
Amen.

The House on the Rock

Little fists, all doubled up. One fist pounding the other, reminding us that we were all builders.

*The wise man built
His house upon the rock
And the house on the rock
Stood firm.*

Then there were Jesus' concluding words from the Sermon on the Mount. "Therefore, whoever hears these sayings of Mine, and does them, I will liken him to a wise man who built his house on the rock" (Matt. 7:24). If we would be wise in life, our teacher said, we must hear what Jesus says. And once we hear what He has to say to us, we must obey. It's the smart way to live.

Now verse two:

*The foolish man built
His house upon the sand,
And the house on the sand
Went **splat**!*

"But everyone who hears these sayings of Mine, and does not do them, will be like a foolish man who built his house on the sand" (Matt. 7:26). Foolish man — a foundation on sand. Wise man — a foundation on rock. Both men hear Jesus. The wise man does what He says, the foolish man doesn't. I caught that, even as a three year old.

Now, everyone on the chorus:

> *The rains came down*
> *And the floods came up (3X),*
> *And the house on the rock*
> *Stood firm.*
> *The rains came down*
> *And the floods came up (3X),*
> *And the house on the sand went —*
>   well, you know.

Dear Lord, I wish some of our preachers today would go back to Sunday school! Some folks actually preach that if you listen to Jesus you can keep the rain from falling. That is not what Jesus said! The rains *will come down*. And the floods *will come up!* Jesus said so. But He also promised that when the waters subside, you and your house will still be standing.

Then there are the other preacher prima donnas for whom perception is everything. If it just *looks* right, then it must *be* right. That's exactly what the foolish man thought, until he heard the first peal of thunder.

▲▲▲▲▲▲

Corrie ten Boom once summarized what she had learned from her years in a Nazi hellhole. She concluded, "There is no pit so deep that He is not deeper still." It's another way of saying that there is no storm so strong that a life founded on Christ is not stronger still. *A life built on Jesus and His words will outlast any storm.* I learned that in Sunday school.

I'm sure I haven't
seen my last flood, Lord. But
each previous storm only lets me see
again how firm a foundation You are,
my strong Rock! "For in the time of trouble
You shall hide me in Your pavilion; in the
secret place of Your tabernacle You shall
hide me; You shall set me high upon a
rock" (Ps. 27:5). Praise be to the
Rock of my salvation!
Amen.

Spanky's Little Rascals

It was time for the "really big shew," as Ed Sullivan used to say. I was about to hit the big time. My Sunday school class was rolling down the street toward television station KOTV, channel 6, the CBS affiliate in Tulsa. This would be my premiere TV appearance!

Being on TV — that was thrilling enough. But we were going to be the audience for my favorite show, "Spanky's Little Rascals"! Hal Roach's prize actor from his "Little Rascals" and "Our Gang" series, Spanky McFarlan, had grown up and moved (of all places) to Tulsa. Yes, friends and neighbors, it was true. Alfalfa's sidekick, Buckwheat's buddy in those hilarious short comic films, and one of the best child actors ever, had moved to *my home town!* Spanky was alive and well and doing kids' TV in Oklahoma.

Every day after school I would faithfully watch Spanky's show, along with the "Mickey Mouse Club" (what red-blooded American boy can ever forget Annette?) the "Howdy Doody Show," and Pinky Lee. But now I was going to crawl inside that box; I was gonna be on TV!

My heart raced as Mrs. King turned the corner to the

station and all us little rascals from Sunday school piled out of the car. We walked into the studio and, brother, what a surprise! That set looked *huge* on TV. But, in real life, it was just a little corner. And, I thought it was a *real* kids' clubhouse. It was just a backdrop. What a letdown. It wasn't as big, it wasn't as inviting, it wasn't as *real* as I'd envisioned. Disappointment. Big time disappointment.

Then, just a couple minutes before we went on the air, out came Spanky. He was a nice enough guy, but his boyhood poundage wasn't that cute anymore. For the first time to my eyes, he looked a little ridiculous. After all, a grown man wearing knickers and a beanie. Then Spanky coached all us kids on exactly when to laugh, when to clap, and when to yell. You mean all that stuff wasn't spontaneous?

The world's glamour, up close, just wasn't all it was cracked up to be. The coziness of Spanky's clubhouse was really only the blare of hot lights. The excitement was canned. Even the laughs were on cue. What a letdown.

I wondered if *glamour* was the right word to describe my first brush with the surreal world of hype. According to the dictionary, it fits perfectly. Glamour, it says, is a romantic, exciting, and often *illusory* attraction.

My Sunday school teacher just wanted to give us a fun

afternoon. She gave me a whole lot more: my first injection of a healthy skepticism of glitz.

Thank you, Mrs. King.

Forty years later, we live in a media-drenched world. Hype is the new norm and Spanky has taken a back seat to mutant creatures. It seems the "New Little Rascals" can only get laughs with bathroom humor. And yet, though it's almost drowned out by the weirdness, you can still hear the faint, deep longing for reality. You see, *the world's glamour, up close, isn't all it's cracked up to be.* I learned that from a lady who taught Sunday school.

*When the lights
go out, the microphones are
silent, and the cameras no longer
record, wading through society's muck of
the flamboyant and superficial, I find You.
Even on the worldwide information superhigh-
way, there's still only one straight, narrow
highway to holiness and rest for our souls. As
the theologians say, You are ultimate reality.
Fame is both illusory and fleeting. I'm so
glad, Lord, that across the years, You
abide, constant, unchanging, full
of grace and truth. Amen.*

Love on Its Knees

The day I saw love on its knees was the day I broke my arm.

It was springtime, 1959. All the guys in the neighborhood were playing "army." Somehow, in one of those freak accidents, I fell and landed the wrong way. I walked inside crying, my wrist sagging almost through my skin. I was close to panic, but my mother was calm.

Praying all the way to the hospital, her one hand was on the steering wheel and the other on my throbbing wrist. Only a few scenes survive in my memory; a brief talk with the doctor, being on the operating table, an injection, swift sleep.

I remember the next scene vividly. I awakened in the middle of the night in a hospital bed, my right arm in a cast. I would have been frightened, wondering where I was, except for a familiar scene that quelled all fear. There was my mother, kneeling at a chair by my bed, praying for me.

My mother, like most back in the fifties, was a stay-at-home mom. I had known her as a comforter when I was sick, a corrector when I disobeyed, a cook when I was hungry.

Storyteller. Chauffeur. Sunday school teacher. Church pianist. Practical theologian. Hostess to visiting missionaries and ministers. Advisor. Friend.

When I later read of Suzanna Wesley, Lillian Shibley seemed like a twentieth-century version. Suzanna, also a pastor's wife, was mother to 17 children. (My mother got off somewhat easier with three.) But both were intercessors.

Suzanna's children knew not to bother her when she sat down and threw her apron over her face. It was her time alone with God. Similarly, I had watched my mother carve out time from her busy schedule to be with the Lord. And I recall how she filled our home with songs of praise as she went about her work.

That night at the hospital I watched her deprive herself of sleep so she could fill the role of faithful intercessor. I'm grateful for the many blessings I enjoy today, including a fabulous wife who prays through the lives of our children. Yes, I'm grateful, but remembering that night in the hospital, I'm not surprised.

◆◆◆◆◆◆

No sight that night could have been more comforting than the assurance of my mother's prayers. Now, I'm privileged to travel the world training pastors to evangelize their respective nations. Often the conditions are perilous. But I know that behind me is an unseen team of those who pray for me, including my wife and my mother. *A personal intercessor is one of life's great treasures.* I learned that from one wonderful lady — my Sunday school teacher, my prayer partner, my mother.

*It's never
been hard for me to obey
Your word to honor my parents.
Thank You for such a godly mother
and dad. Am I planting the same legacy
for my sons? As the song says, may those
who come behind us find us faithful;
faithful to You, faithful to them, faithful to
our covenants, faithful to intercede. Thank
You, Lord, for models through the years
of faithful intercessors. Keep
building new models. In Jesus'
name. Amen.*

It's Against Our Religion

I still remember the sting of embarrassment sitting in the corner of the gym. The quizzical looks from my classmates. And my sigh of relief that there was one other kid who was handing a similar note to our teacher.

"Please excuse David from dancing instruction. It's against our religion to dance."

Even then my moderating tendencies against this brand of too serious fundamentalism were beginning to show. Hey, we're talking eight year olds *square dancing* here, for Pete's sake!

So my sons never knew that kind of ostracizing embarrassment. Am I happy about that? I'm not sure.

Oh, of course, I'm glad that my whole worldview got broader and that I came to realize that God was probably far more amused than offended at third graders learning to square dance. I'm glad that I learned that some forms of dance are (and always have been) acceptable and even biblical parts of worship. I'm enormously glad that unflinching *religion* has given way to a nurturing *relationship* between God and me.

So, yes, it was a little much to embarrass a kid over such a superficial thing. Yes, we were probably wrong to insist on non-participation. But I am forever grateful that, even though I came to have a broader view than my parents regarding dancing, their view was *consistent and sincere.* It was a natural expression of what the entire message of their lives was about; they just wanted to please Jesus.

By the time I was ready for my senior prom, my dad was home with the Lord. My mother probably wasn't in a position to restrain me from going. I don't recall that she tried. On my own, I chose not to go. By then, I was concerned about my testimony and the consistency of my Christian witness.

Although I pray Naomi and I are as committed to Christ as our parents were, I'm glad our children grew up in a little freer environment. But I trust our sons haven't been deprived of something that's crucial to spiritual development. You see, beliefs that aren't worth standing for aren't a very big deal.

Yes, my folks probably chose the wrong issue on which to take a stand that cost them (and me) something. But they did it for all the right reasons. We may look back with a few enlightened laughs, but no regrets.

△△△△△△

We are entering a time again in America when standing for our faith will cost us something. The cross of Christ, according to the Bible, is a *scandal*. One of the best ways to prepare our children for the future is to teach them that if they don't stand for something, they will fall for anything. Drawing the line on square dancing may be a little ridiculous. Drawing the line on the cross of Christ isn't. *It takes courage to stand up for your faith.* It's an important value for the future that I learned in the past, in Sunday school.

*Lord, I want
to thank You for parents
who were more concerned with
my spiritual development than my
social development. I was in no way
slighted. "No good thing will You withhold
from those who walk uprightly." (Ps. 84:11)
My folks believed that. And You have once
again proven true to Your word. I love
You, Lord. Thank You for memories
with many more smiles than
tears. Amen.*

Robber's Cave

So many life-altering decisions happen at Christian camps. They were (and are) an extension and reinforcement for what Sunday school teaches all year. Our church's summer camps provided the environment for two important landmarks for me. In 1959, I invited the Holy Spirit to fill and control my life. In 1965, two weeks before my father died, I made an unqualified dedication of my life and future to God.

The setting for both experiences was a campground our church rented in the summer close to Robber's Cave State Park in the mountains of southeast Oklahoma.

In the summer of '59, I was happy, trusting, and open to God's touch on my life. At the night service I sat on the old wooden bench and sang the songs of Zion as sweet breezes danced through the pavilion. Then, behind the shouting voice of the preacher, I heard the soft, tender voice of God's Spirit.

Kneeling down at an old-fashioned altar and "tarrying" for God's power might be consider *passé* today. But what was transacted with God that night opened up a whole new realm of communion and fellowship for me. Walking back to the cabin, well after midnight, I felt I was walking on air. I drank in the smell of the pines and looked up at the stars. I had just had an experience with the Creator of all I sensed. I had encountered the *living God!*

"Don't be drunk with wine," Paul told the Ephesians, "but continue to be filled with the Spirit, speaking to one another in psalms and hymns and spiritual songs, singing and making melody in your heart to the Lord" (Eph. 5:18-20). Even as a boy, I understood what he was talking about, not theologically but *experientially*.

In Romans 12 Paul urges believers to "present your bodies to God as a living sacrifice." In the summer of '65 at Robber's Cave, as my dad was 150 miles away battling for his life, I did exactly that. Once again, Scripture moved past sterile doctrine. I *encountered* God and His call, and obeyed.

Back when Oklahoma was Indian Territory, Robber's Cave was where notorious bandits hid from the law and justice. Robber's Cave was where I came clean.

▲▲▲▲▲▲

Years later in seminary I would hear a rather odd, faddish term. They called it *doing theology* or *incarnational theology*. At nine years old, I couldn't have spelled it or defined it. But in the summer of '59, I had some close encounters of the spiritual kind with a living, loving Jesus that made all I knew externally *about* Him a throbbing explosion of reality within me. I found out, *the Holy Spirit wants to be real to you.*

Wonderful

*Lord Jesus, I praise You
because You are the same
yesterday, today, and forever. You
never change and You want to be just as
real, just as close, just as personal today as
in those "fiery bush" landmark experiences
long ago. Make every intersection of my
life today an altar of consecration and
worship. In Your exalted name.
Amen.*

The Baptists Are Havin' a Revival!

Remember the kid I told you about who stayed out of dancing instruction with me? His name was Randy, my third grade buddy.

One day he came up to me, and blurted excitedly, "David, my church is having a revival. I want you to come!"

Randy was a Baptist. I was a third generation Pentecostal. But, the Baptists were havin' a revival! And I wanted to go. When I asked my dad if I could go, he was quick to say yes. (Thank you, Dad, for demonstrating unity in the body of Christ in that one little "yes.")

That night Randy's parents drove us to the Winnetka Heights Baptist Church in Tulsa. And was I in for a surprise. In fact, I was pretty shocked! Not so much in how different this church was from my own, but in how similar it was to mine.

These Baptists — they were singing a lot of the same songs we sang. (You mean Fanny Crosby wrote songs for them, too?) And the evangelist — he was telling about the same Jesus; with the same gospel story! I felt right at home because in the singing, in the testimonies, in the preaching — there was the cross, front and center.

I still remember that people responded that night when the preacher asked people to come and be saved. There were tears, confession, and forgiveness. People were meeting the very same Jesus I loved — right there in the Baptist church!

It was one of my first lessons in appreciating that "there is one body and one Spirit, just as you were called in one hope of your calling; one Lord, one faith, one baptism; one God and Father of all" (Eph. 4:4-6).

In Sunday school, Mrs. Highfill had put heavy emphasis on a single word when we learned John 3:16. "For God so loved the world, that He gave His only begotten Son, that *whosoever* believes in Him should not perish but have everlasting life." I remember the same impression from another memory verse, Revelation 22:17. "*Whosoever* will, let him come and take of the water of life freely." Jesus can show up in the most surprising places. Sometimes, He even shows up in church — other peoples' church, no less!

When Randy's folks dropped me off at home later that night, I was a little wiser. Even though we didn't agree on everything, I knew there was a *really big* number of people in my town who loved and followed Jesus. And together, we had a *really big* story to tell.

▲▲▲▲▲▲

For years Charles Spurgeon's mother prayed for his salvation. One day, in answer to her prayers, he was gloriously saved. Later, Spurgeon's godly, Methodist mother told him, "Son, I recall many times asking the Lord to save you, but I never recall asking Him to make you a Baptist."

"Mother, isn't that just like the Lord?" the great preacher responded. "He gave you exceeding abundantly above all that you asked!"

Yes, *lots of Christians love the same Jesus you love.* I learned that in Sunday school, and at the Baptists' revival.

*Thank You,
Lord Jesus, for the
beauty, diversity, strength, and
tenderness that comes through in the
many expressions of Your body, the
Church. Your body, Your bride. How
beautiful Your Church is to You. May the
whole Church be beautiful to us, as well. So
often, Lord, Your body bleeds not from the
attacks of outsiders, but from self-
inflicted wounds. Forgive us and heal
us. Make us one, that the world
may believe. In Jesus' name.
Amen.*

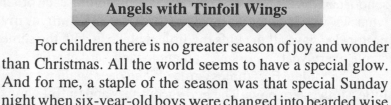
For children there is no greater season of joy and wonder than Christmas. All the world seems to have a special glow. And for me, a staple of the season was that special Sunday night when six-year-old boys were changed into bearded wise men and giggling girls became angels bedecked in bedsheets and tinfoil wings.

It was a night of transformation. A little church stage became the City of David. Somehow, the hue of a blue light bulb resembled that holy night on the Judaean hillside. And there were other miracles. People we hadn't seen all year suddenly appeared in the pews. And when the tinfoiled angels sang, the hard hearts of adults became soft.

The center of attraction was an inanimate little doll, tucked in flannel, "lying in a manger." As amateurish as all this was, somehow there was a touch of glory on it. Indeed, that Baby caused an intersection between heaven and earth.

Suddenly, kids who only saw each other twice a week shared a mystic bond. We played instruments, sang about God coming down to earth, and quoted those wondrous Christmas verses.

And then suddenly, it was over. We were at the Sunday

school party in the fellowship hall, excitedly telling each other what we were hoping to get for Christmas. That night, my pastor-dad gave all the kids the little white bag with the same staple every year: an orange, an apple, and hard candy.

The Middle East tunics came off and once again we were little Midwestern boys. The bed sheet robes and tinfoil wings were carefully packed away for next year's performance.

So, I guess we weren't wise men and angels after all.

Or were we? Just as surely as the wise men discovered Jesus, so had we. And just as surely as real angels proclaimed His birth, so did we. Just as surely as angels had visited shepherds, God had visited us. And whether we wore a scout uniform or tinfoil angel wings, we knew — *you can have God's touch on your life.*

Our churches' Christmas pageants today are high tech productions, complete with strobe lights, computer-generated backdrops and angelic choirs flying 30 feet overhead. Some churches even risk camels down the aisles (for "realism," they say). But for me, I'll never forget the annual night of wonder when the props were minimal and yet — heaven met earth. It's part of my rich heritage from Sunday school.

Precious

Jesus, I'm so glad that on

those chilly December nights in the

recesses of Christmases past we had

something so glorious to celebrate. You were

in our corner, You were God for us, God

with us, and God in us by faith. And

You still are. Praise the name of

Jesus!

A World Outside of Tulsa

My 11-year-old eyes had never beheld anything more awe-inspiring. Mr. Hopkins' station wagon, chock-full of fifth grade, aspiring major leaguers, was driving up to the biggest structure I had ever seen. The five-hour drive had been worth it. There it was, rising like a colossus, the stadium that was home to the old Kansas City Athletics. I'd never seen anything close to that huge in my hometown. Oh, sure, our Tulsa Oilers farm team was fun to watch. And the thousand or so people who showed up were still pretty impressive. But *this* . . . this was literally a whole new ball game!

Bill Hopkins had been my Sunday school teacher for over a year. I'd heard him patiently try to explain how the 12 tribes of Israel had really important meaning for our young lives. But for me the half-tribes of Ephraim and Manasseh stayed entombed in ancient (and pointless) history.

But today Mr. Hopkins wasn't wearing a tie. The first thing I saw on his head wasn't Brylcream, but a baseball cap. Bill Hopkins had stepped out of Canaan and was leading us to a far more glorious promised land — the visiting New York Yankees dugout!

Awestruck, I suddenly realized I was shaking hands with

Yogi Berra. Quickly my young mind went to work: "Yogi Berra was with the Yankees when Joe DiMaggio was still on the team. (He must have shaken hands with DiMaggio.) DiMaggio was a rookie when Babe Ruth was still on the team. (DiMaggio must have shaken hands with Babe Ruth!)

All of a sudden, this Oklahoma boy had joined a line of divine succession. I stood speechless, watching another Oklahoman, Mickey Mantle, make balls disappear high over the center field fence in batting practice.

Later that night at the game my eyes witnessed history. I watched a shy, nice guy named Roger Maris belt a line drive over the fence. It was one of 61 home runs he would hit that year; a record that has stood unchallenged for over 35 years.

As we drove back to Tulsa, I realized that my heart and my head had been permanently stretched. You could go past the minor leagues to the majors! Cities like Kansas City existed that dwarfed Tulsa. And my hand — *my* hand — had been linked with the immortals.

▲▲▲▲▲

You see, all I need to know — all of the essentials for successful living — I learned in Sunday school. And one of the big lessons I learned from Mr. Hopkins is this: *You can play in a bigger world.*

*Thank You, Lord,
for Sunday school teachers
like Bill Hopkins — teachers who
pull back the curtain so a young person
can get a glimpse of just how big Your
world really is; and see that it's possible to
make a major league contribution to Your
purposes in that world. And thank You for
teachers who know how to "hit a home
run" outside the classroom as well
as inside. Amen.*

As I recall, the Canary Choir sang this song to the tune of *Stand Up, Stand Up for Jesus.* We sang,

A little child of seven, or even three or four,
May enter into heaven through Christ, the open door.
For when the child believeth on Christ the Son of God,
'Tis then the child receiveth salvation through His blood.

As it was with their parents, both of our sons received Christ as little children. I'm glad they trusted the Lord Jesus early for salvation. Now I want them to trust Him for everything else.

In a nation that brutalizes its offspring in so many ways, the least we as Christians can do is give these precious children the gospel. I believe in child evangelism. Statistics are on its side. Some studies indicate that 19 out of every 20 Christians receive Christ before the age of 25. After that, the odds against conversion are astronomical.

I've never met anyone who is sorry he or she came to Christ early in life. I've encountered many who are sorry they didn't.

Shortly before his second-century martyrdom at age 95,

the Early Church father Polycarp testified, "Eighty-six years have I served the Lord." That means Polycarp must have come to Christ as a child. Eighteenth century Bible expositor Matthew Henry was converted at the age of six, hymnwriter Isaac Watts at nine.

Young children are notably tender. Their sincerity is never in doubt. Their heart attitudes contribute to genuine conversion. In fact, Jesus told adults they have to assume the posture of a child to experience the new birth. "Unless you are converted, and become as little children, you will by no means enter the kingdom of heaven" (Matt. 18:3).

Jesus himself is the greatest proponent of child evangelism. In Matthew 18:1-14 He pronounces a stinging curse on anyone who offends a child who believes in Him. He considers it possible for little ones to "believe in Me."

The great Bible teacher G. Campbell Morgan said, "A vision of and desire for the kingdom of God is the master passion in all work for children." Morgan called Mark 10:14 the "Magna Carta of Children." There the Lord commands, "Let the little children come to me, and do not forbid them; for of such is the kingdom of God." Jesus was careful to use the word that literally means very little child. No one was to be excluded.

One of my fondest remembrances of my father-in-law and mother-in-law is watching them in their Awana vests, sitting in kiddie chairs at their church, lovingly teaching preschoolers. They were in their late seventies.

I end these light-hearted reminisces with a very serious appeal. If we're at all concerned about the future of our nation and world, we'd better reach children for Jesus.

Begin with the children in your house. Move on to share the gospel with other children you influence. Keep on, wrapping arms of love around the hundreds of wounded children all around you. And then, stretch further, to embrace an entire generation who are desperate for God's love.

▲▲▲▲▲▲

We must judge our lives' effectiveness in light of this question: What are we doing to influence the *next* generation for Jesus Christ? *It matters what happens to the next generation.* And that is why there is something called *Sunday school.*

*Life's
greatest treasure is You.
Oh Lord Jesus, for Your sake, help
me lead the next generation to the
treasure. I'm so glad that Almighty God
enjoyed holding and blessing children. Like
You, may I always love the little children.
Help me to bulldoze every roadblock
that keeps them from coming to
You. Amen.*

Now, Let's Review

Everything I need to know I learned in Sunday school. Here are some wonderful truths I learned:

1. People matter, because they are made in the image of God.
2. You can never run away from God's love.
3. Jesus is a friend of sinners.
4. The message of Jesus is wonderful good news.
5. Open your heart to Jesus.
6. Joy is spelled "Jesus, others, and you."
7. Only Jesus can bring love and hope.
8. God doesn't play favorites.
9. You can spread the sunshine of God's love.
10. The Bible is God's book and your guide.
11. You should serve your country by being a good citizen.
12. Live for what matters, and what matters is the exaltation of God's Son to the ends of the earth.
13. A life built on Jesus and His words will outlast any storm.

14. The world's glamour, up close, isn't all it's cracked up to be.
15. A personal intercessor is one of life's great treasures.
16. It takes courage to stand up for your faith.
17. The Holy Spirit wants to be real to you.
18. Fellow Christians love the same Jesus you love.
19. You can have God's touch on your life.
20. You can play in a bigger world.
21. It matters what happens to the next generation.